Artful Angels

Reflections - Paintings

Mary Montague Sikes

Thank you for purchasing an authorized edition of *Artful Angels*.

High Tide's mission is to find, encourage, promote, and publish the work of authors. We are a small, woman-owned enterprise that is dedicated to the author over 50.

When you buy an authorized copy, you help us to bring their work to you.

When you honor copyright law by not reproducing or scanning any part (in any form) without our written permission, you enable us to support authors, publish their work, and bring it to you to enjoy. We thank you for supporting our authors.

High Tide Publications, Inc.
Deltaville, Virginia 23043
www.HighTidePublications.com

Printed in the United States of America
ISBN: 978-1-945990-88-5

Angels Everywhere

Although I don't recall ever seeing an angel, I have always felt their presence. Sometimes when I close my eyes, I feel one standing next to me.

Now, the artist within me sees angels and paints them. In this book, I have included a few of those angels and the words received intuitively about each one.

You will notice that I use many different materials to create my angel paintings. Some are watercolors; others are acrylic. Part of the collection is painted with artist pastels or with mixed media. I even have one that evolved using oils and encaustics. My angels come in many sizes, from very small, 4" x 6", to rather large, 54" x 42". Most are on watercolor paper or Yupo. Four are painted on stretched canvas.

Sometimes, it is helpful to open this book to a painting and simply meditate about it. Silence is a friend. Perhaps an angel will appear in the quiet of your day. Take a deep breath and discover the majesty of angels all around.

Mary Montague Sikes

Your Angels

As you view the following images, you might discover an angel that I did not see in the forms and colors I created.

You might want to turn this book around and view a painting from a different angle.

Perhaps you will encounter a flurry of angelic images no one else has found or seen.

Perhaps new words will fill your mind with love, hope, and understanding, and you will write them down.

These words and images were created to inspire meditation, new beginnings, and new perception of the angels all around us.

Select just one and see what it tells you.

Angel of Majesty

Angel of Majesty, light flows 'round you like rain.
Stars shine through your transparent wings.
The silver shoes you wear lie hidden in the mist.
Pastel colors cloak your shoulders.

You are beauty; you are goodness.
Energy surrounds and compels you to fly higher.
Do you reach out to save us from falling?
Or do you lunge upward towards the stars?

From my window I watch for you.
Sometimes I send my troubles into the night,
Hoping you will find them in the shadows
And hurl them far away from me.

Majesty and magic prevail as you travel
Through the clouded dark night sky
Into the massive channels of the universe.
Following your starlit trail would bring me joy.

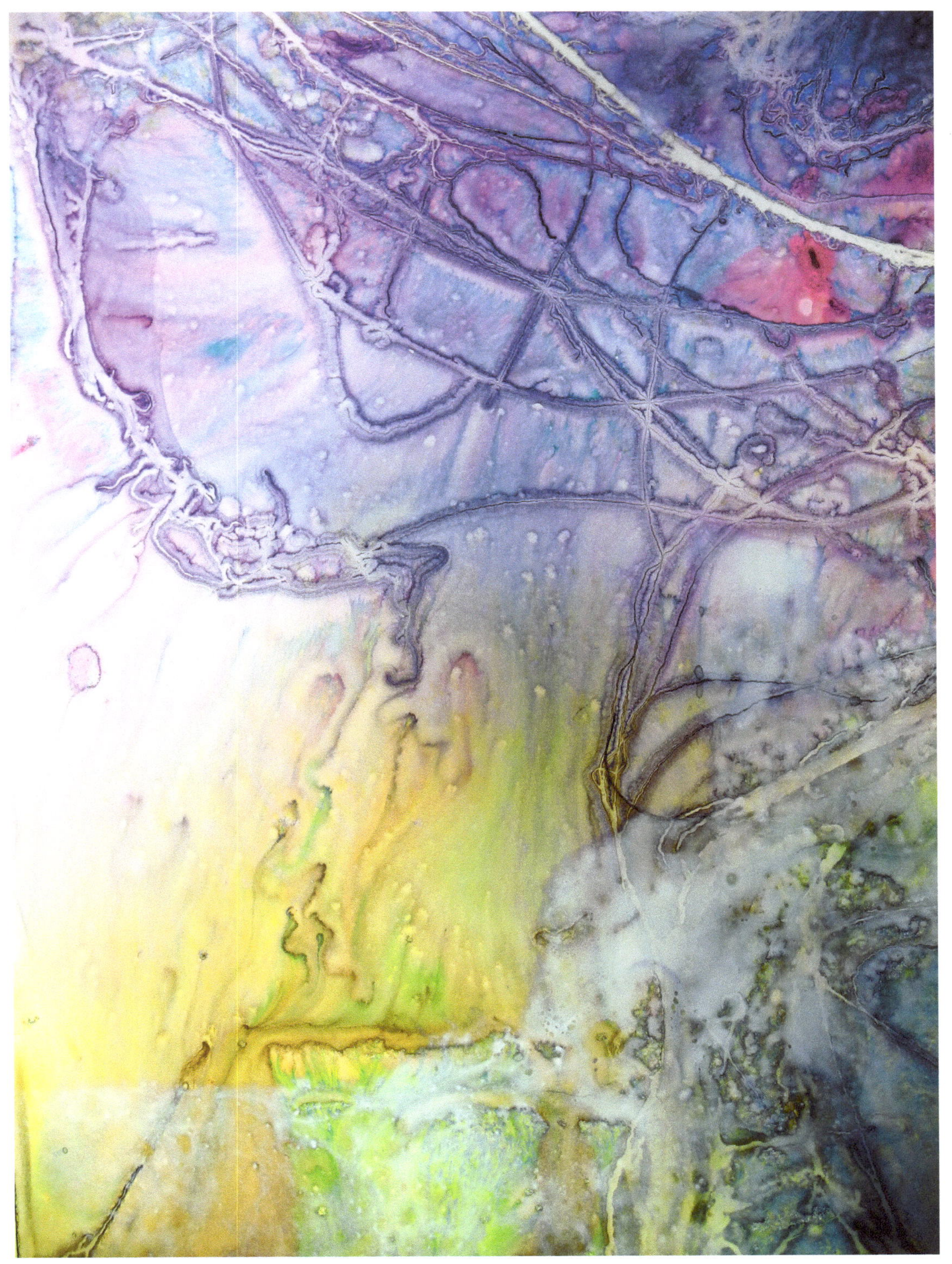

Angel of Earth and Sky

Angel of the Earth and Sky,
You are the angel I seldom see.
You dance on tiny feet
And point upward to the stars.

When I see your reflection in the water, I smile.
It's not your reflection at all.
Instead, bubbles of light twirl inside the pool
Propelling afar rays of colored charm.

Blue, purple, aqua spiral into the universe.
Joy beyond imagination brightens our world.
You live not on this sad, silent plane.
Instead, you ascend above into the far unknown.

Bright heavens surround you with love beyond belief.
Enormous lights swell above your halo.
Imagination thunders forth like a mighty sword,
But, unlike you, it cannot touch the essence of the night.

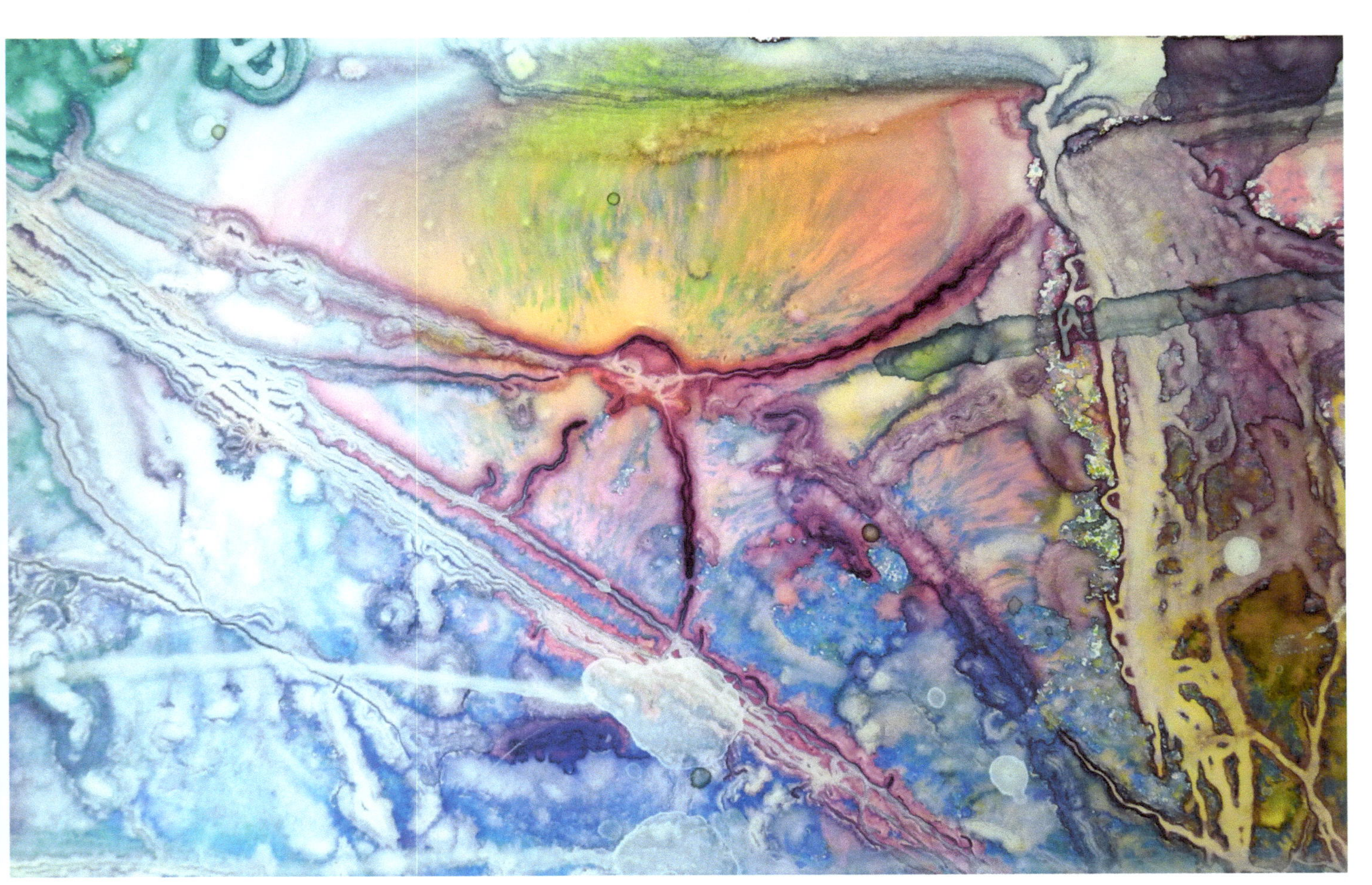

Angel of the Ice Lake

Angel of the Ice Lake,
You are invisible.
The icy blue covers your veil.
Are you there and I just can't see you?

Sometimes you flit through the sunlight.
I see you then, but you fly away too fast.
Are you the guardian of the lake?
I like to think you are.

We all need guardians
To protect us when we call out.
When you appear through my violet lens,
I will follow you into warm pure waters.

Thank you for being by the ice that ebbs and flows.
Sand once edged the shores and young hands touched the water.
Now old hands laced with veins search the ice mounds
For signs of lost days and the once-seen angel.

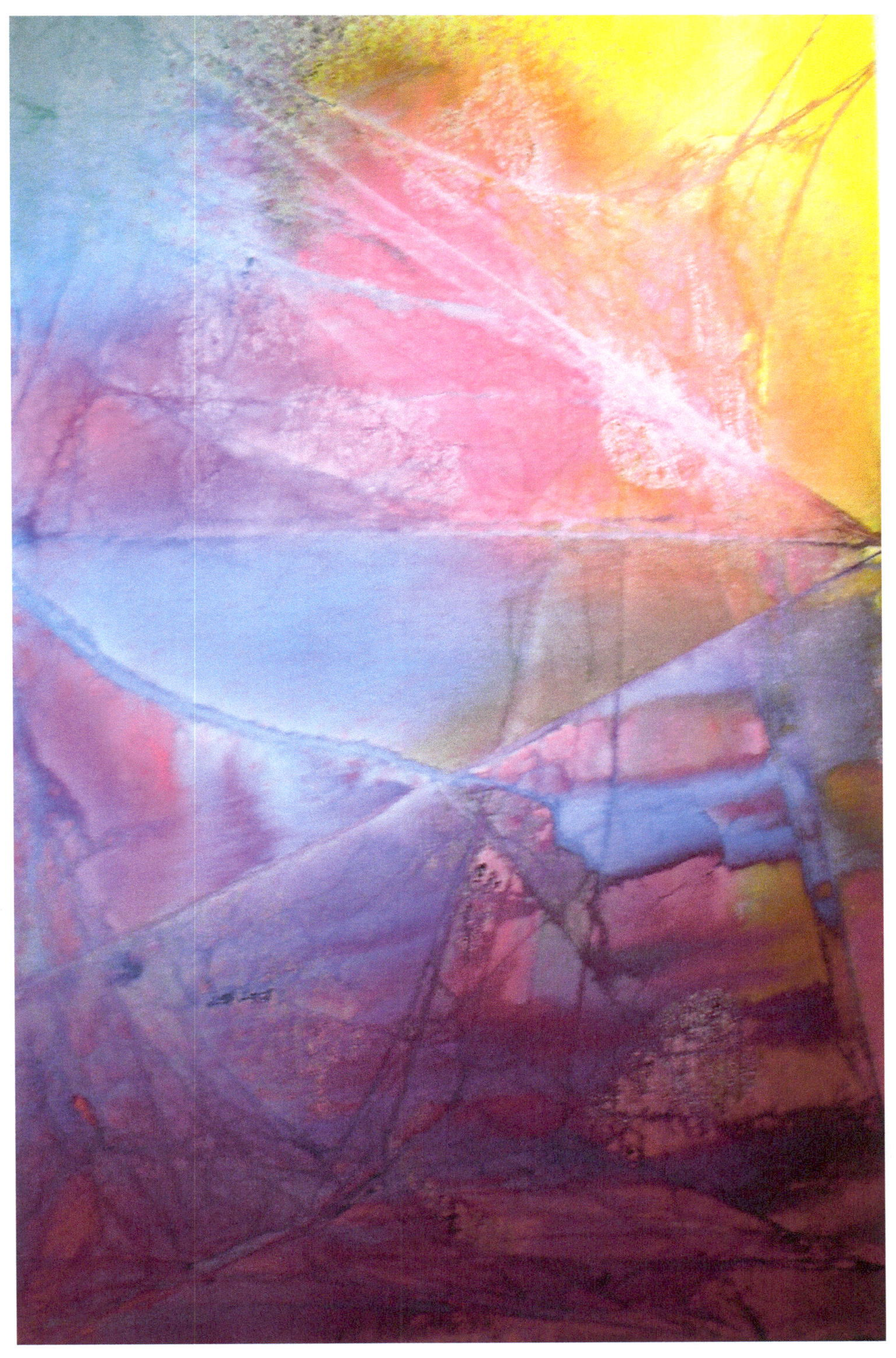

Angel of the Crimson Shawl

You stand with your back to me.
I cannot see your face.
But I know that you guide me
To that space faraway, yet so close.

The air that surrounds you is sweet and heavy.
It presses hard against me, so I can hear you speak.
Sometimes I listen as you sing into the night
With a glorious sound that warms and embraces me.

You are the angel that calls out to me.
And I shall follow until you turn your face.
Then I shall know the secret of the angel of the crimson shawl.
At long last, I shall be where I belong.

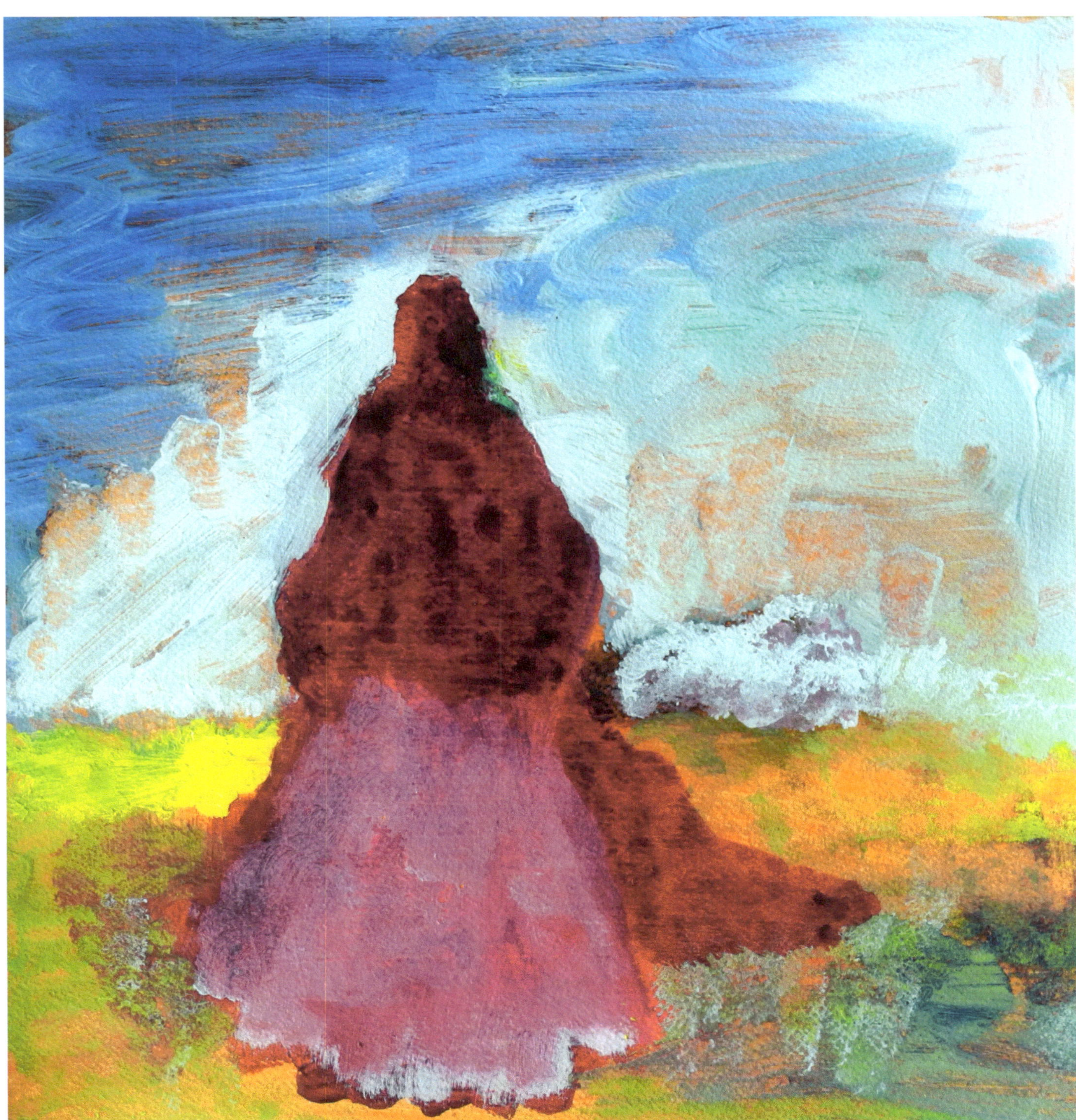

Beneath Angel Wings

Beneath Angel Wings I see fire and ice,
So volatile the rivers flow.
Clouds gather with angels hidden there.
Bright, vivid memories flood my open heart.

Joy shines in violent light.
Treasures bloom in heart's desire.
I spread my arms to draw them in,
So many angels to fan the flames.

Watching the fire leap higher,
I clutch the heat against my chest.
Inside my mind I will not forget
The hovering presence of angel wings.

Flames thunder and roar.
My hands reach out
To claim the energy for my soul.
Angel wings fade into the night.

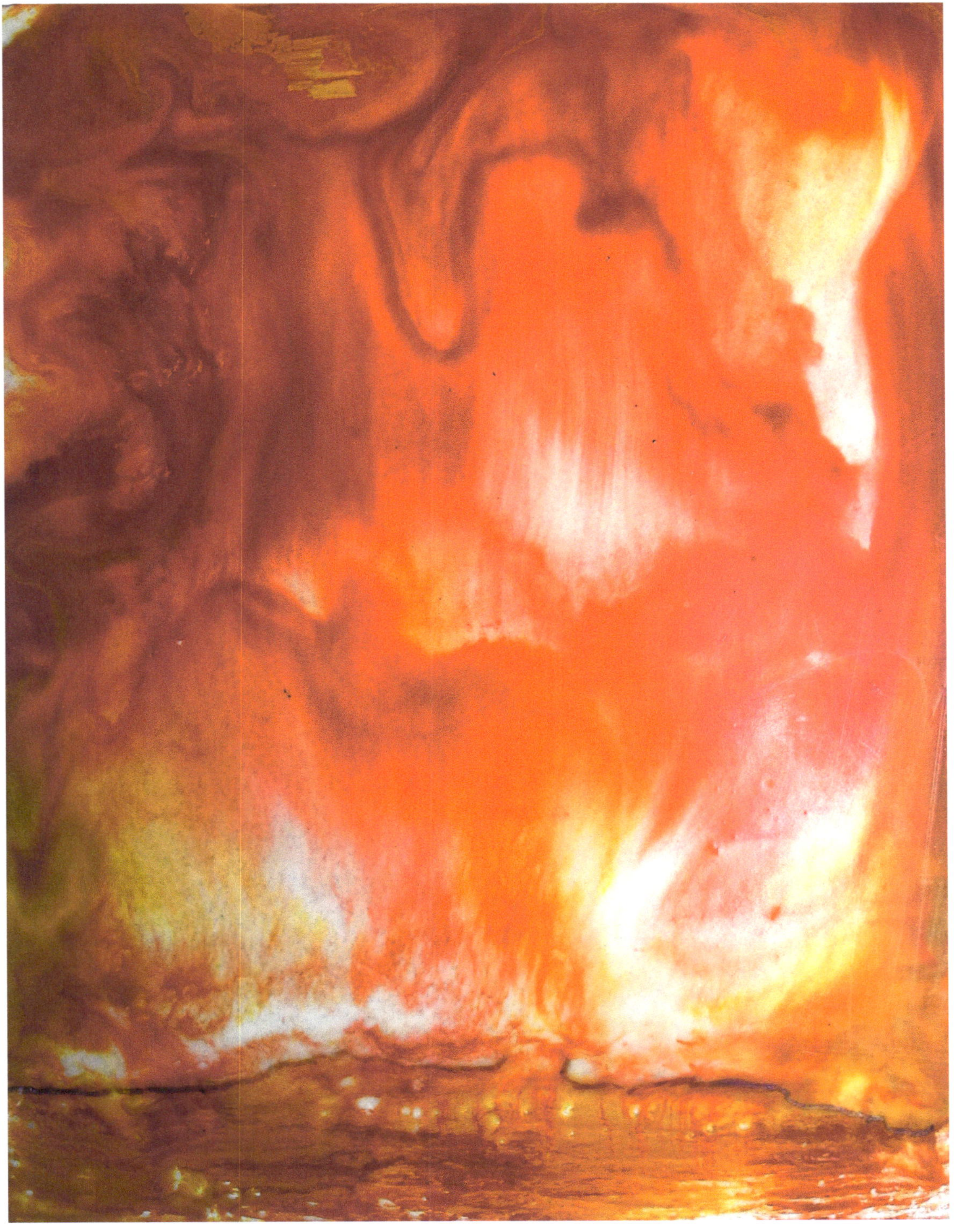

Angel of Xanadu

My Xanadu Angel sings loudly from pink and purple clouds.
She comes from the land of complete perfection.
Where love and light abound.
It is a place where she is seldom needed.

Many angels live on Xanadu.
The people there are angels.
Long ago, they earned wings of trust and faith.
Only good walks the streets of that planet.

Sometimes one angel appears here just for fun.
She sprinkles loving stardust on Planet Earth.
She brings sparkle and sunshine to the darkest day.
She turns a tiny corner into Xanadu on Earth.

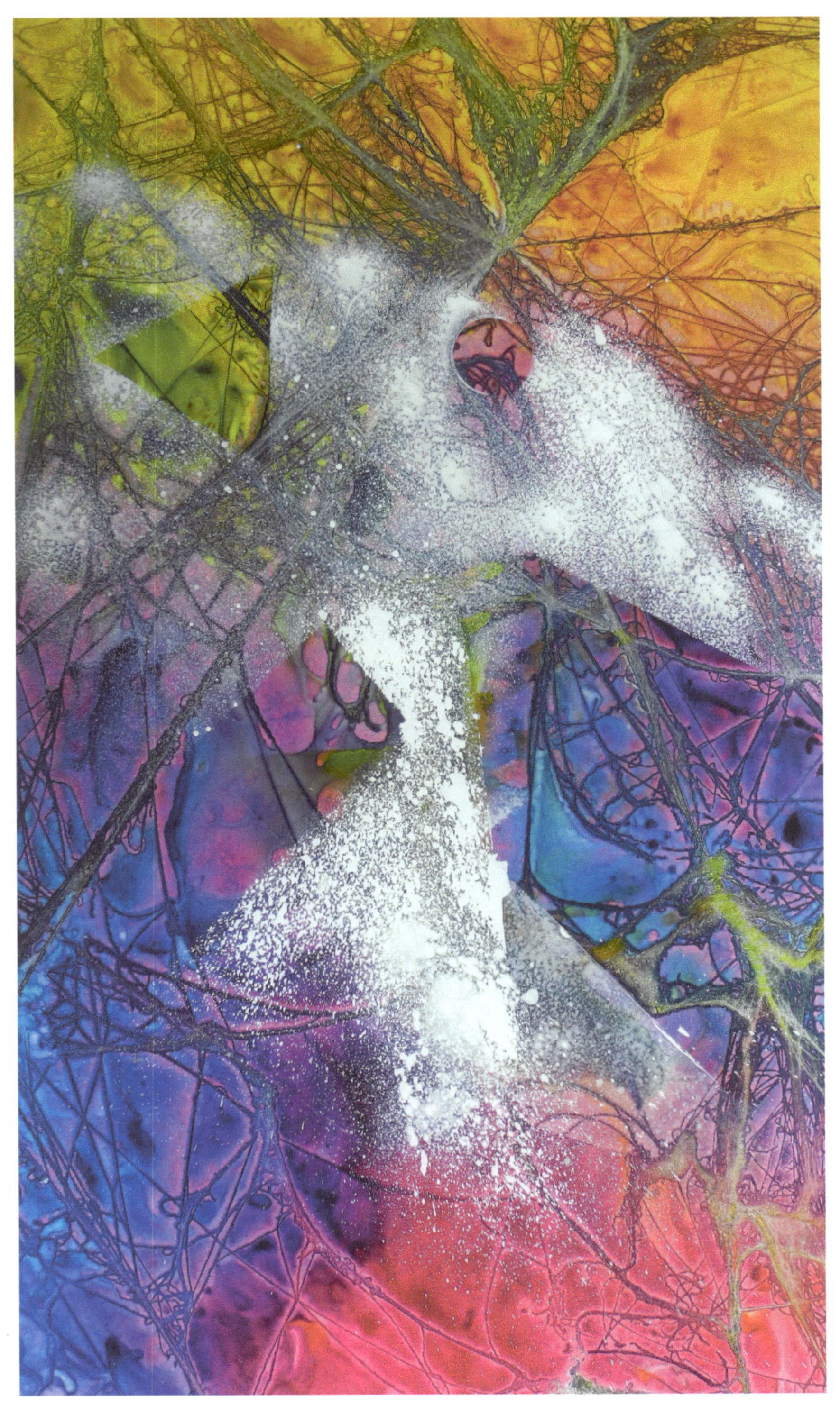

Angel at the Window

There is an angel at my window.
Sometimes I hear her knocking.
Her lips are always moving
But I cannot grasp her words.

I must listen harder.
I know she beckons me
To follow her into the night
And find where she is leading.

She points to a path of glowing rocks.
She holds a light in her hand.
One day I shall reach out
And follow where she is guiding me.

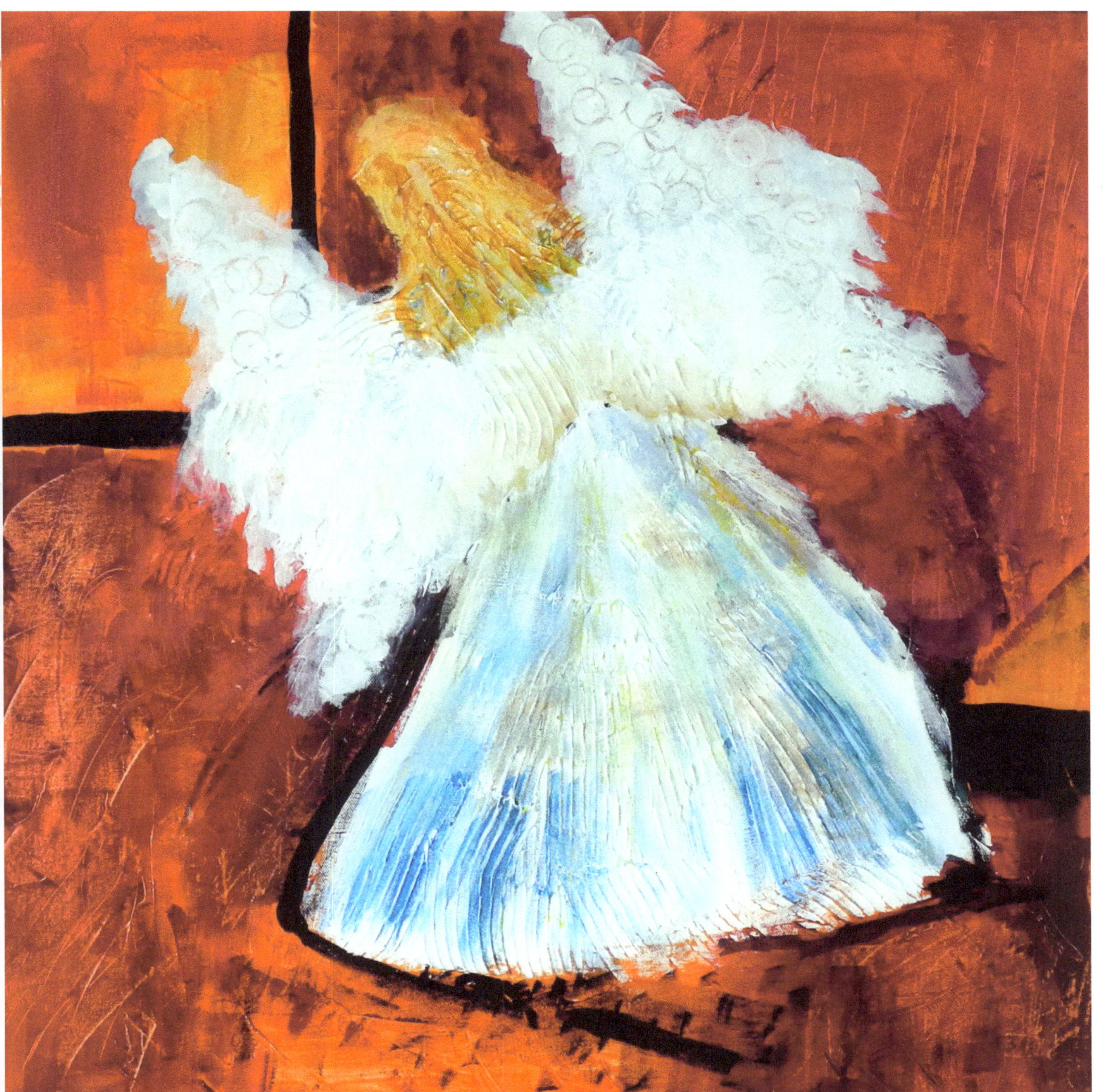

Twin Angels in the Prism of Life

You look like stained glass,
My Twin Angels.
How did you find me?
Were you flying among the stars?

I think you were hiding inside the clouds,
Shrouded in phthalo green dust.
That is a favorite color of mine.
Did you know that?

Twins like you fascinate me.
Especially when color hides you,
When prisms of purple surround
Your flight into the night.

I believe you are a beam of light,
Sent to lead when I need you,
Gliding in on diamond wings
That I will remember forever.

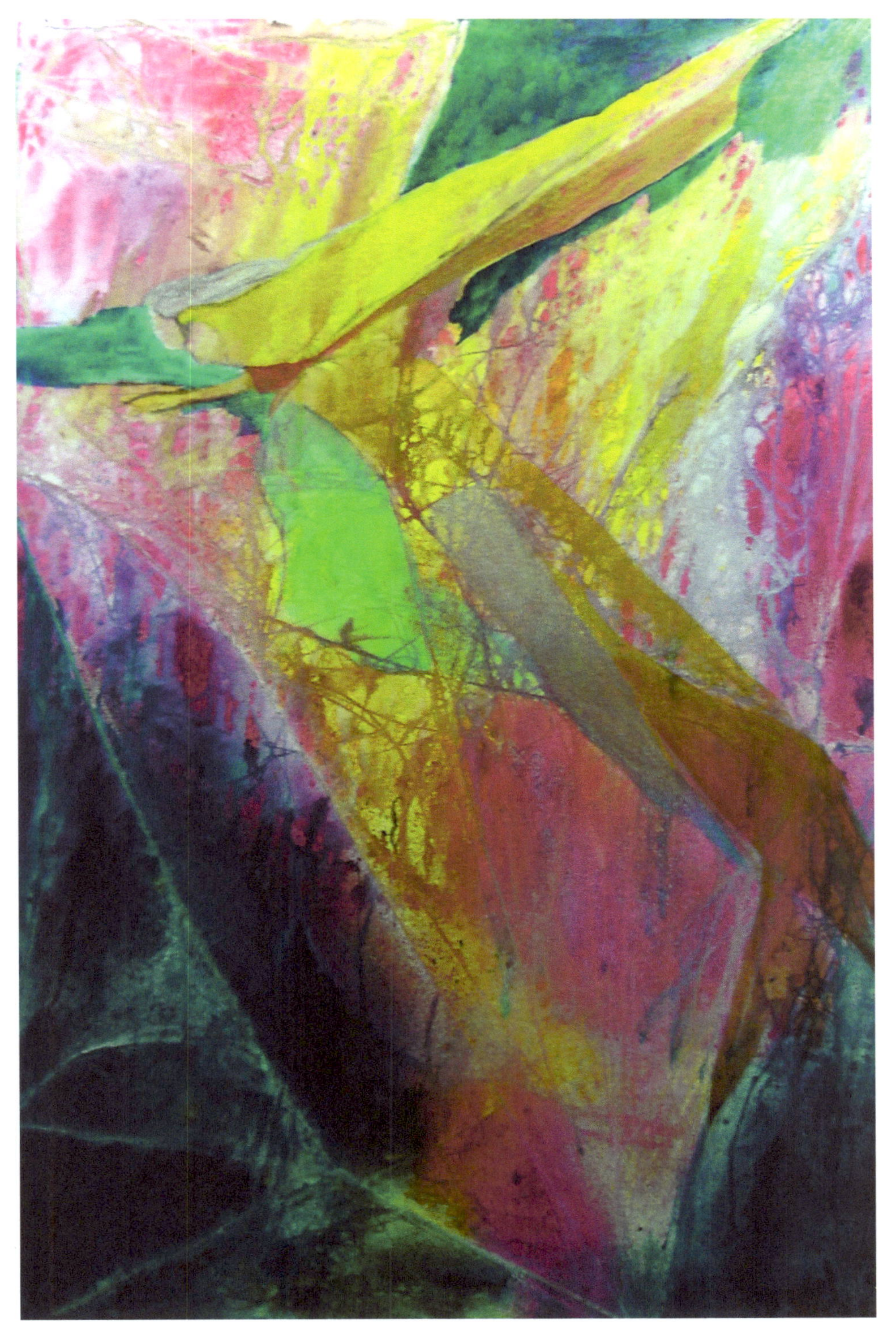

My Angels

Sometimes I long to create my own unique angel. It is at those times that I retreat into my art studio and pull out a variety of painting materials.

Often, a destination from my travels inspires me, such as the hillside cathedral in Arizona red rock country. With vivid memories of a hot day among the colorful rocks, I created the painting, "Angel of the Holy Cross". Photographs I took on several trips to Sedona helped as I worked. I used my favorite Rembrandt soft pastels to draw and paint my very special angel.

Other times, I put away the pastels and worked with acrylic paints, brushes, and palette knives to develop my angels that appear in larger paintings, including "Angel of the Marshland". The ever-changing marshes I see from my writing studio window provided the inspiration for this painting as did the "Tapestry for Peace" project angel I created for the National League of American Pen Women.

Sometimes I like to imagine texture in the angel I'm painting. "Angel and Cherubs of the Starry Night" features a textured angel with a Van Gogh sky in the background. At that time, I was enjoying Seward Johnson sculptures based on Van Gogh paintings that were on loan in Key West, Florida.

There is something mystical about watercolor. My "Angel of the Timeless Garden" has an air of mystery surrounding her. Painted with traditional watercolor, this is an angel I imagine living among the plants, flourishing in a garden of abundance. "Angel of the Sunshine" is another watercolor bathed in yellow light. Yellow makes me happy and so does this angel.

Occasionally, my love of design comes out in an angel I paint. That is especially true in "Angel of the Silver Cross". Captured in an acrylic painting, this angel is guardian of our bedroom. With her watching over us, I feel safe and protected.

Which came first, the angels or the words? Sometimes the words babbled forth as the paint brush filled with vibrant color. Other times, I studied the finished painting and waited. The words flowed quickly and in abundance.

Please take your time and meditate on the paintings and words in this book.
Perhaps you will see and draw your own angel–maybe even the guardian who guides you.
Perhaps words will come to you, and you will write. Breathe deeply and see what happens.

Angel and Cherubs of the Starry Night

Is it only on starry nights that the angels come?
I look for them on other nights as well.
Cherubs follow some of the angels.
Are they little lost spirits needing a home?

Do angels know the answers of why we are here?
They come to us as guardians, you know.
When least expected, they dance before us
Little cherubs sometimes in tow.

Some folks shy away from angels.
They are frightened by shiny spirits.
But when tiny cherubs come with them
There is less reason for alarm.

Sometimes I look for the Angel of the Cherubs.
She is tall and kind.
Someday she will take my hand and lead me
As she does the cherubs into another realm.

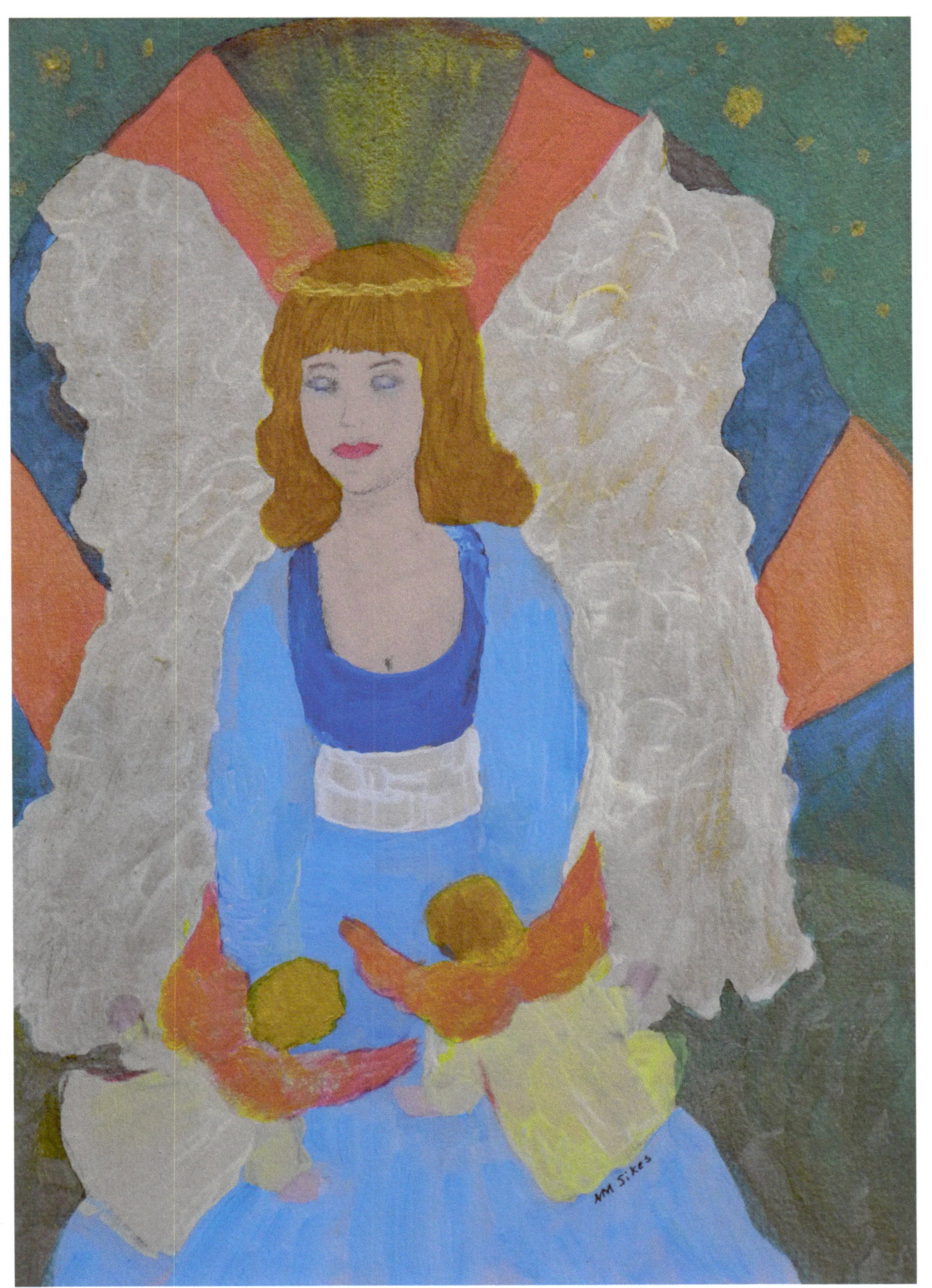
AM Sikes

Angel of the Timeless Garden

Angel of the Timeless Garden,
I hear you call my name.
So sweet a voice,
So gentle a song.

I wish to dance and sing in your garden.
The loving words of your verses call to me
And I flutter like a butterfly into the flowers.

The beauty that surrounds you
Is like none other I have seen.
The colors are beyond what I can paint or see.
The sounds are more than I can hear.

Thank you for leading me to this pure garden.
Thank you for the vivid truth forever present there.
You are the angel of sweetness.

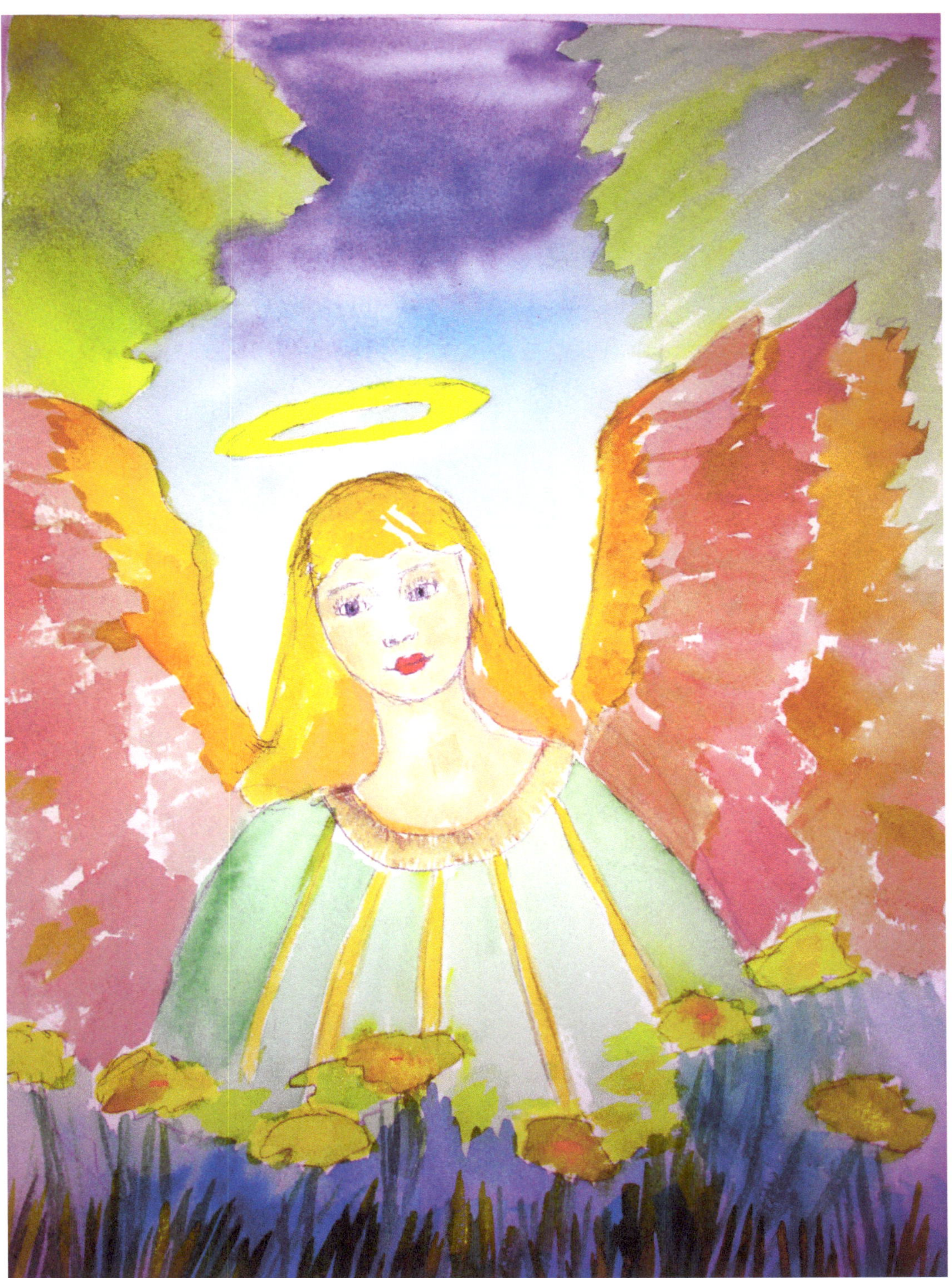

Angel of the Marshland

Angel of the Marshland, your colors amaze me
And you have such a vibrant glow.
Like lost among the brown grasses
You've changed the colors to suit you.

I love the trees and the waters of the marsh.
Do you hide there often?
I will look for you next time I go.
Then, I'll touch your golden hair.

Your wings are lovely.
They have a greenish shine
And you hold a sash of gold
Within your tiny hands.

Please stay inside the marshland
Until I find you hidden in the grass.
Call to me with your sweet voice.
Let me see you there.

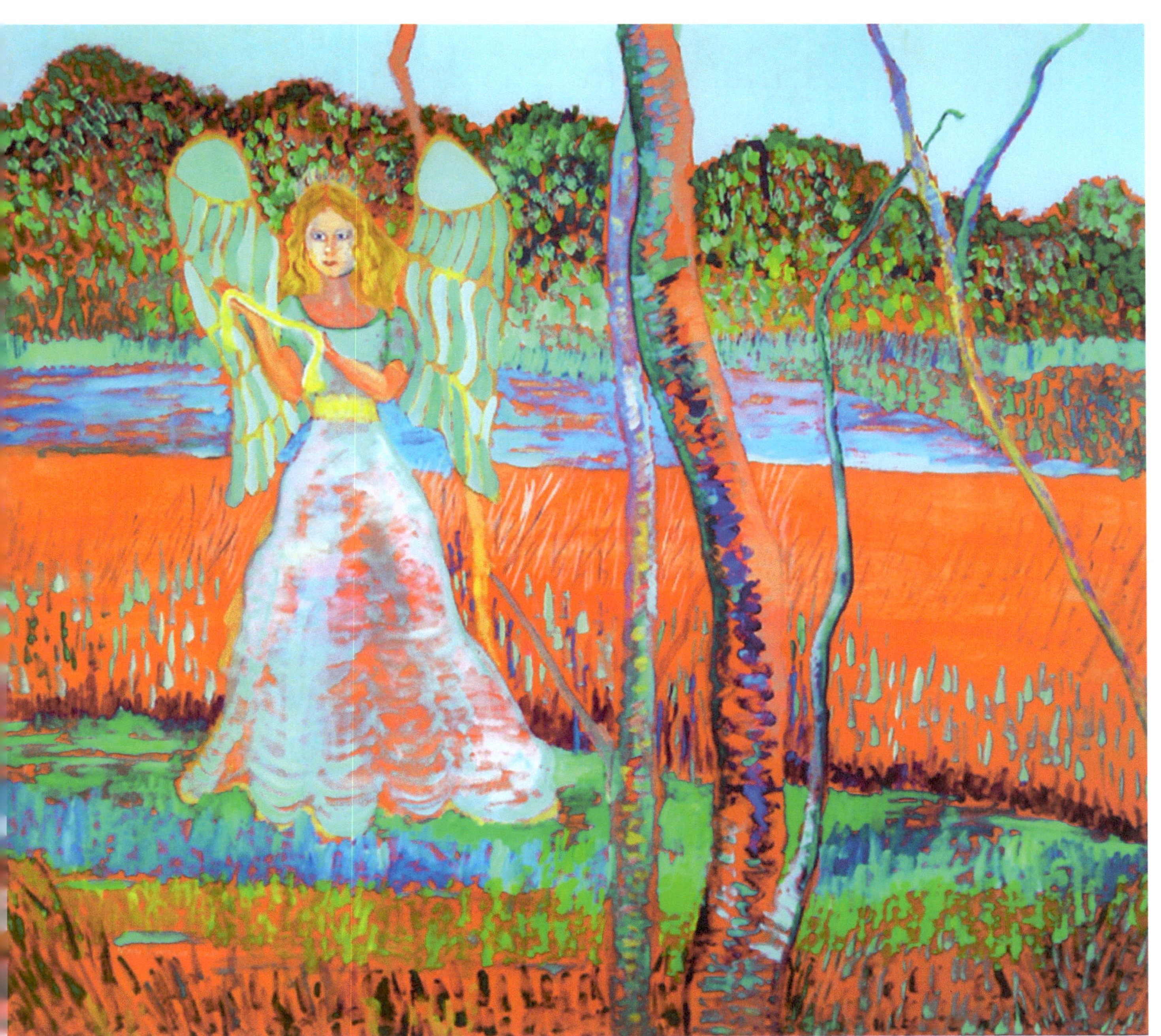

Angel of the Silver Cross

She smiles at me, my angel does,
And gives me hope and joy.
My heart yearns to know the meaning of life.
She laughs and I do not understand.

When the night turns darkest
She takes the bitterness away
And tells me tomorrow will be much better.
Life is what you make it, she says.

This angel leads us to light and love.
She holds the key to our universe--
The one that encapsulates and contains us
Until we are ready to fly out on our own.

Sometimes she reaches to the stars
To give us a greater glow.
Angel of the Silver Cross,
You bring magic as we trek forward with you.

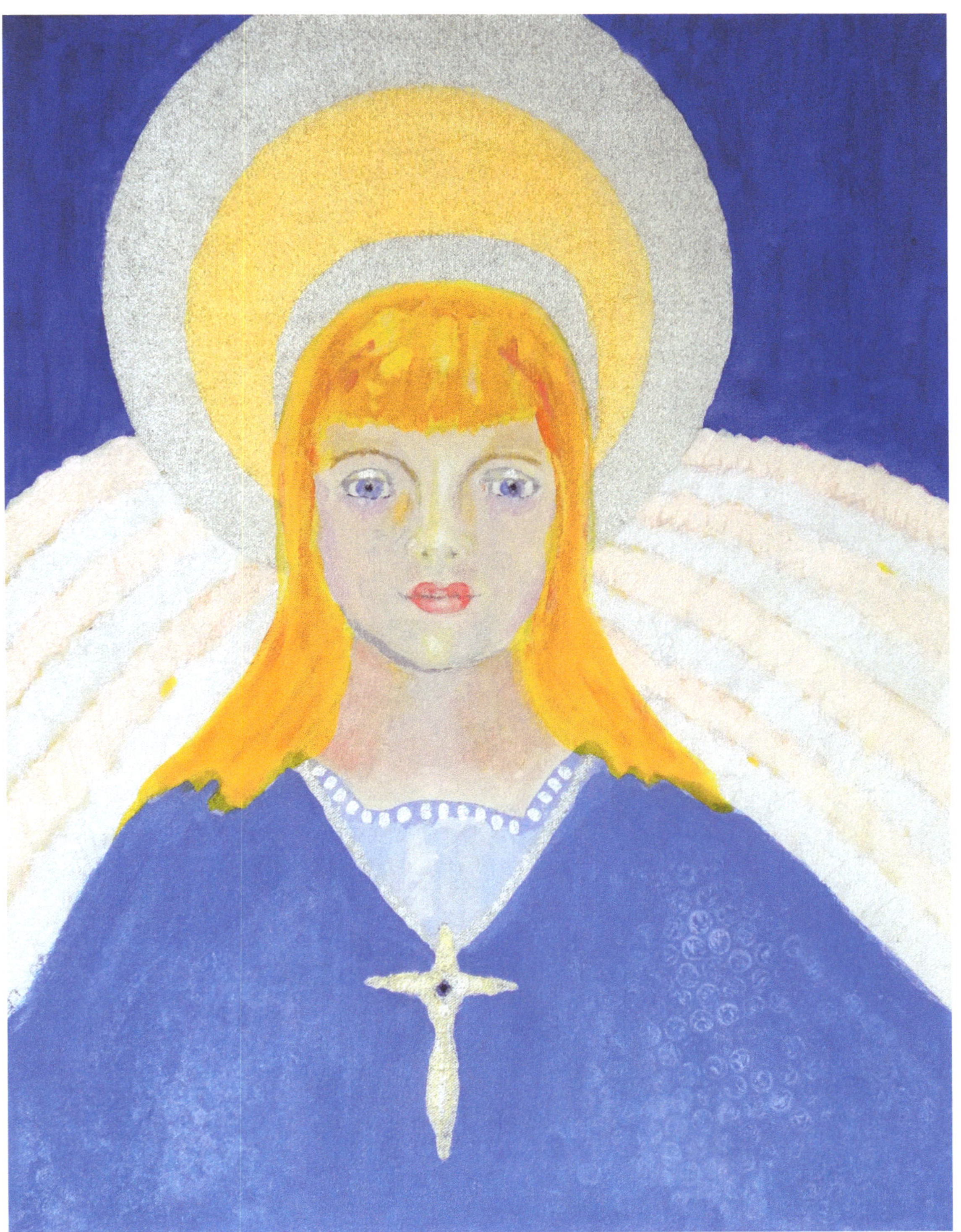

Angel of the Holy Cross

Angel of the Holy Cross,
You take my breath away.
Austere, determined
You are as I wish to be.

I found you there, high on a Sedona hill
In a church that is more than a church
Perched on a hillside
Among the silent red rocks.

So much meaning, so few words
We listen in the quiet
As hushed voices
Drift in dewy wind.

Soundless, somber, beautiful
I hear your call
And feel the strength of your light.
Come with me, I hear you say.

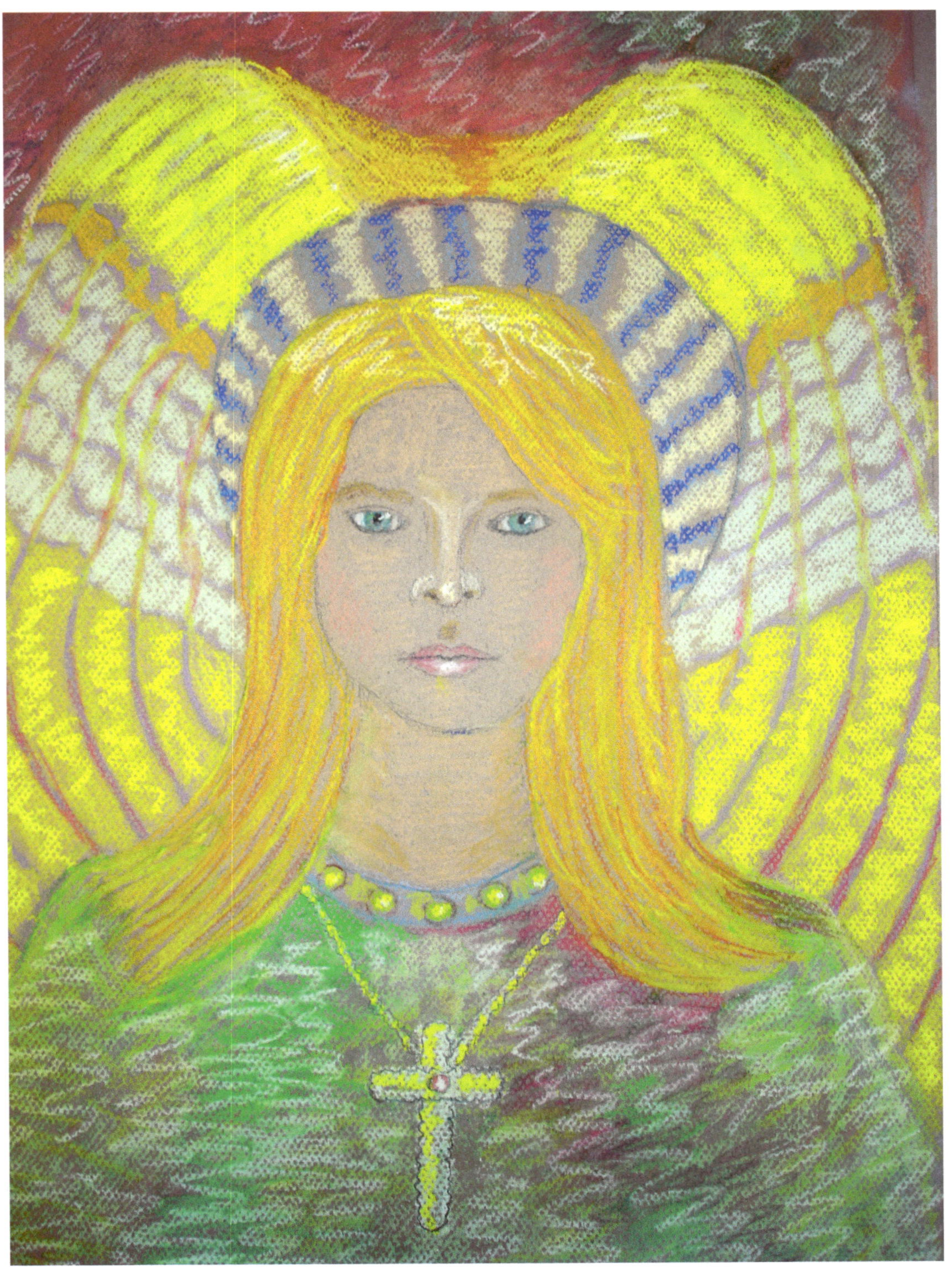

Angel of the Sunshine

Sunlight glistens in your hair.
You fly through the stars at night.
But the glow of daytime awakens you.
Fly high, my angel.

In the fields you flit among the blossoms.
You shine to brighten lonely souls.
Your smile lifts lost spirits and leads them home.
Fly high, my angel.

Yellow grows into a brighter star.
As you float from the darkness
You carry a special light for those who wait beyond.
Fly high, my angel.

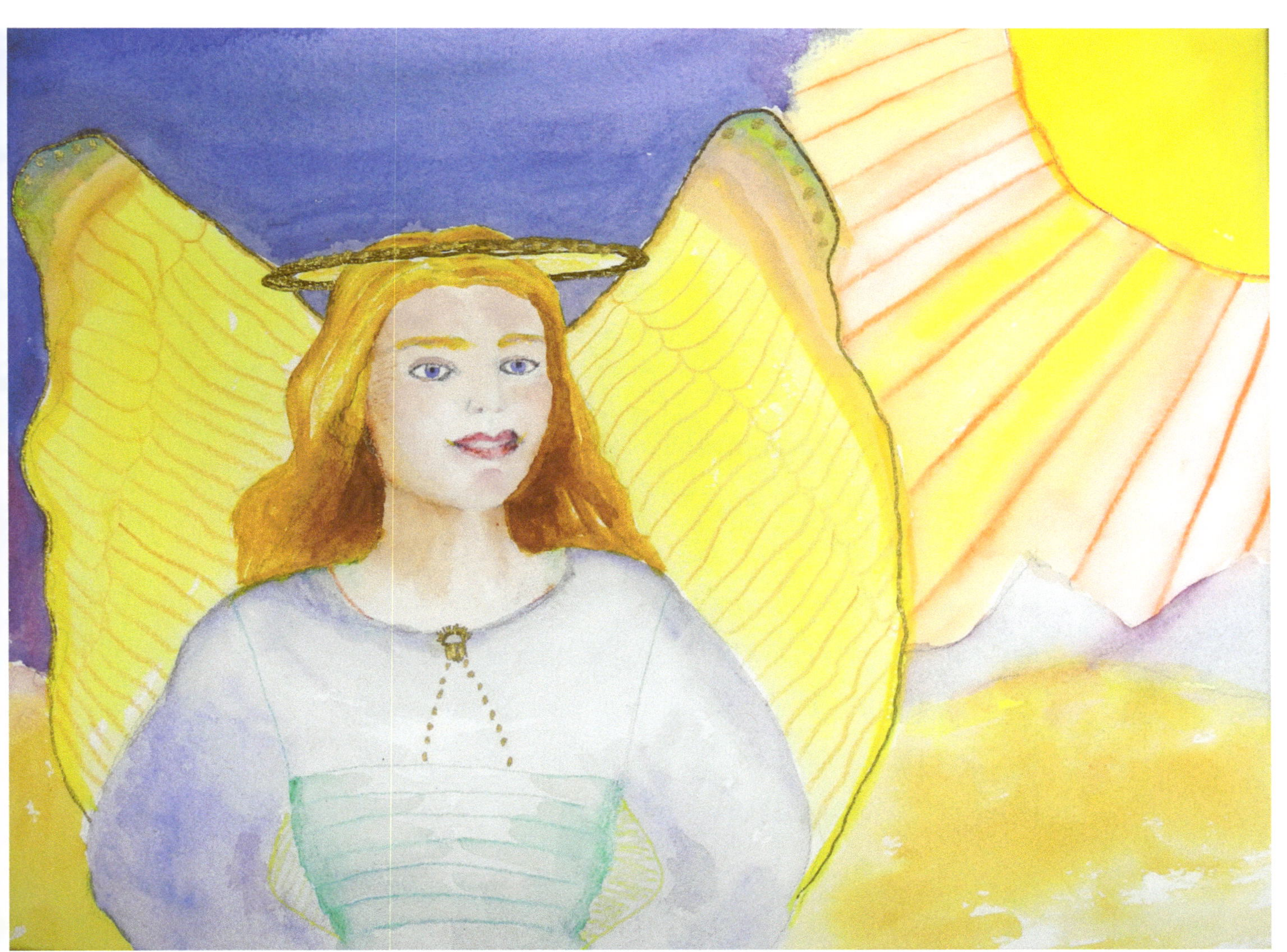

About the Angel Paintings

1. "Angel of Majesty" 10" x 10" Watercolor on Yupo
2. "Angel of Earth and Sky" 4" x 6" Watercolor on Yupo
3. "Angel of the Ice Lake" 36" x 24" Watercolor on Canvas
4. "Angel of the Crimson Shawl" 12" x 12" Acrylic on Paper
5. "Angel and Cherubs of the Starry Night" 14" x 11" Acrylic on Paper
6. "Beneath Angel Wings" 10" x 8" Encaustic on Board
7. "Angel of Xanadu" 30" x 22" Watercolor/Mixed Media on Yupo
8. "Angel of the Sunshine 11" x 14" Watercolor on Paper
9. "Angel of the Holy Cross" 20" x 16" Pastel on Paper
10. "Angel at the Window" 24" x 24" Acrylic on Canvas
11. "Angel of the Silver Cross 20" x 16" Acrylic on Canvas
12. "Angel of the Marshland" 42" x 54" Acrylic on Canvas
13. "Twin Angels in the Prism of Life" 36" x 24" Mixed Water Media/Canvas
14. "Angel of the Timeless Garden" 14" x 11" Watercolor on Paper

About the Artist and Author

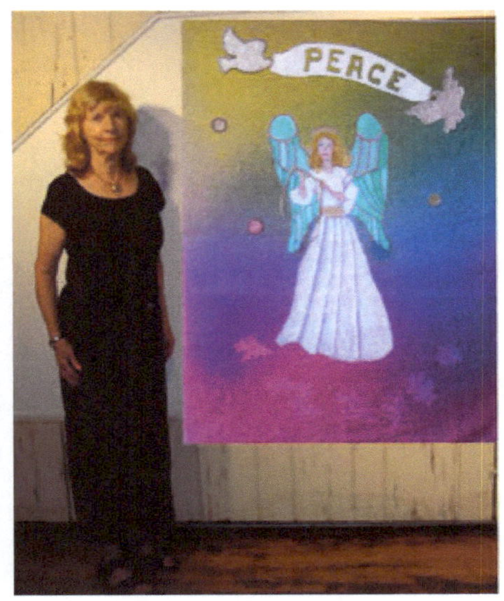

"Angel of the Earth and Skies" ©MMSikes

A few years ago in Denver, Colorado, I met a lovely lady named Eve MacIntosh. When she told me about her vision while traveling on a Florida interstate of a giant angel, holding earth in one hand and a planet in the other, she started me on a new journey painting angels.

"There is a place in space for peace," are the words she heard spoken that day. Those words inspired Eve to create the *Tapestry for Peace* project for the National League of American Pen Women with unique panels coming from branches throughout the United States. I created for the Richmond Branch an angel panel on a piece of linen that Eve supplied.

That angel was one of many I have painted in the years since I met Eve, who, unfortunately, died suddenly a few months after our encounter. Her Denver Branch, NLAPW carried on with her project that was unveiled at the National Conference in Denver in 2006. Now, whenever I paint an angel, I think of Eve and her beautiful vision and mission.

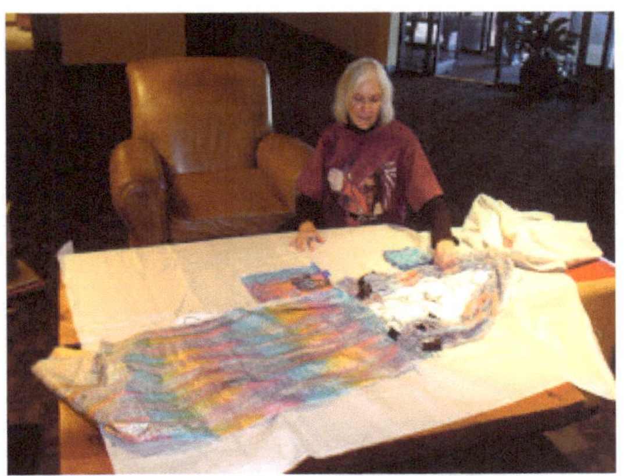
Eve Mackintosh with Tapestry for Peace project ©MMSikes

Besides painting angels, I enjoy working with many subjects and all kinds of art materials, including watercolors on Yupo, acrylics, oils, mixed media, oil and cold wax, encaustics, pastels, and more. Painting and writing for as long as I can remember, my work is influenced by studies with Dr. Joseph Costa and the late Dr. George Ritchie, the works of Dr. Ian Stevenson, and others.

My educational background includes a degree in psychology from the University of Mary Washington, extensive studies in the Art Department of the College of William & Mary, and a MFA in painting from Virginia Commonwealth University. My work is in private and public collections in the United States, Canada, and the Caribbean. It is on view at Crossroads Art Center in Richmond, Virginia, and at Prince George Art & Frame in Williamsburg, Virginia.

Other Books by Mary Montague Sikes

Hearts Across Forever, 2019

Spirit Visions Soul Songs, 2018

An Artful Animal Alphabet, 2017

Evening of the Dragonfly, 2015

Scenic James River, A Snapshot in Time, 2013

Hotel DuPont, A Snapshot in Time, 2013

Williamsburg Inn, A Snapshot in Time, 2012

Daddy's Christmas Angel, 2012

Hilltop House, A Snapshot in Time, 2011

The Jefferson Hotel, A Snapshot in Time, 2011

The Homestead, A Snapshot in Time, 2011

A Rainbow for Christmas, 2011

Published! Now $ell It! 2005

Hotels to Remember, 2002

www.ingramcontent.com/pod-product-compliance
Lightning Source LLC
LaVergne TN
LVHW071630100826
845154LV00007BA/121
9781945990366